HOW MAMAS LOVE THEIR BABIES

WRITTEN BY
Juniper Fitzgerald

ILLUSTRATED BY
Elise Peterson

THE FEMINIST PRESS
AT THE CITY UNIVERSITY OF NEW YORK
FEMINISTPRESS.ORG

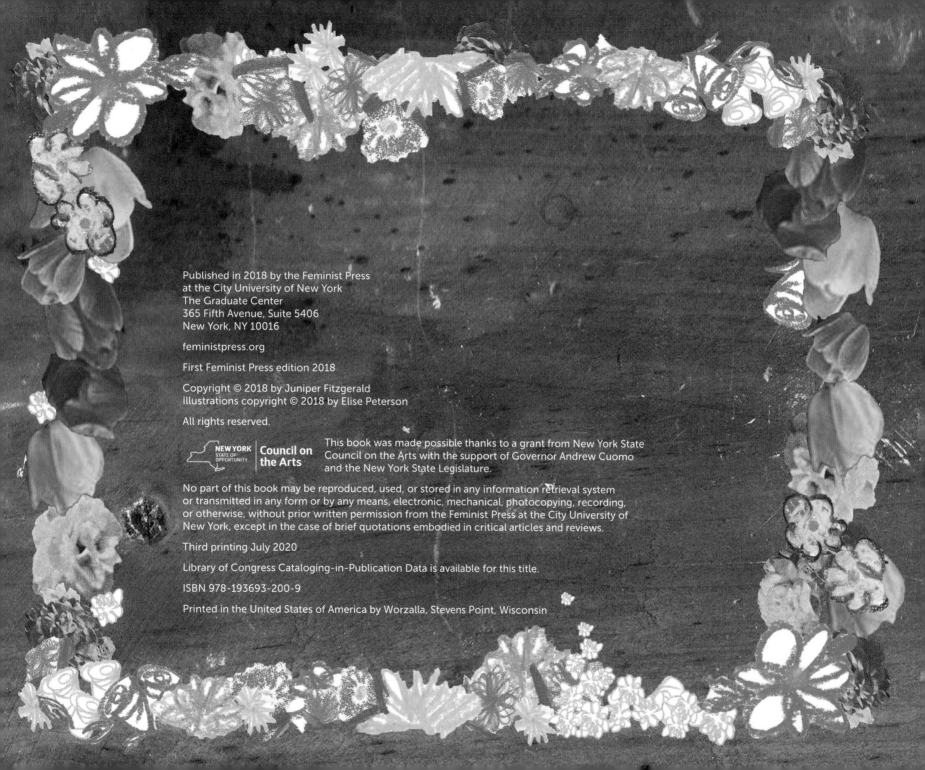

Published in 2018 by the Feminist Press
at the City University of New York
The Graduate Center
365 Fifth Avenue, Suite 5406
New York, NY 10016

feministpress.org

First Feminist Press edition 2018

This book was made possible thanks to a grant from New York State Council on the Arts with the support of Governor Andrew Cuomo and the New York State Legislature.

Third printing July 2020

Library of Congress Cataloging-in-Publication Data is available for this title.

ISBN 978-193693-200-9

Printed in the United States of America by Worzalla, Stevens Point, Wisconsin

FOR WILLA

Babies love mamas …

and mamas love babies.

How do mamas love their babies?

Mamas use their bodies to care

for their babies in so many ways.

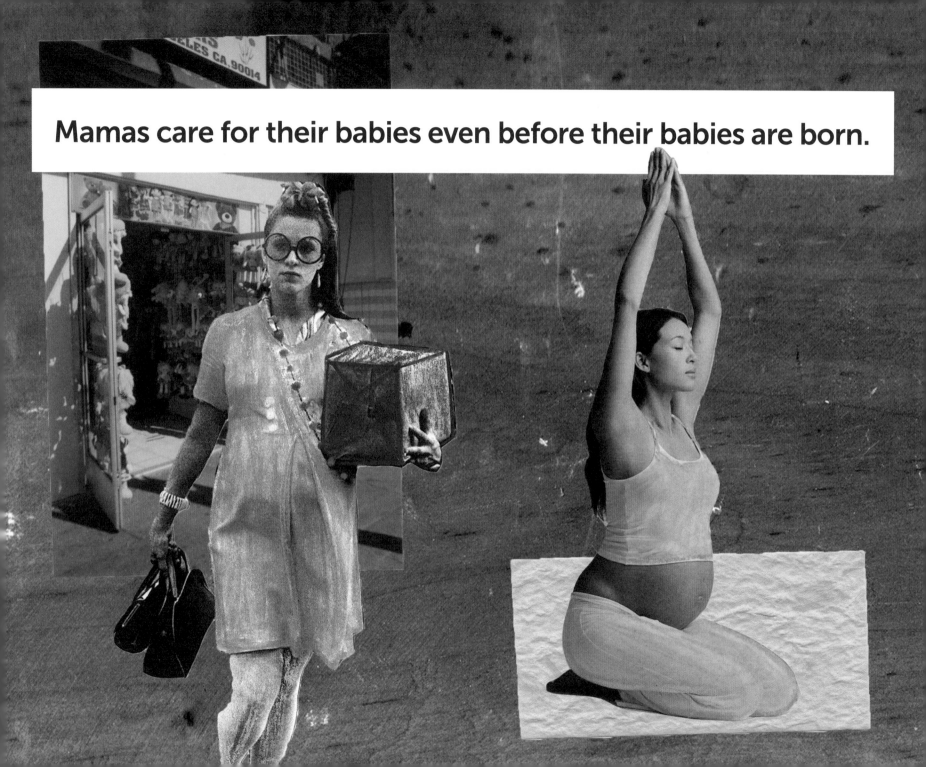

Mamas care for their babies even before their babies are born.

Some mamas care for their babies inside their own bodies.

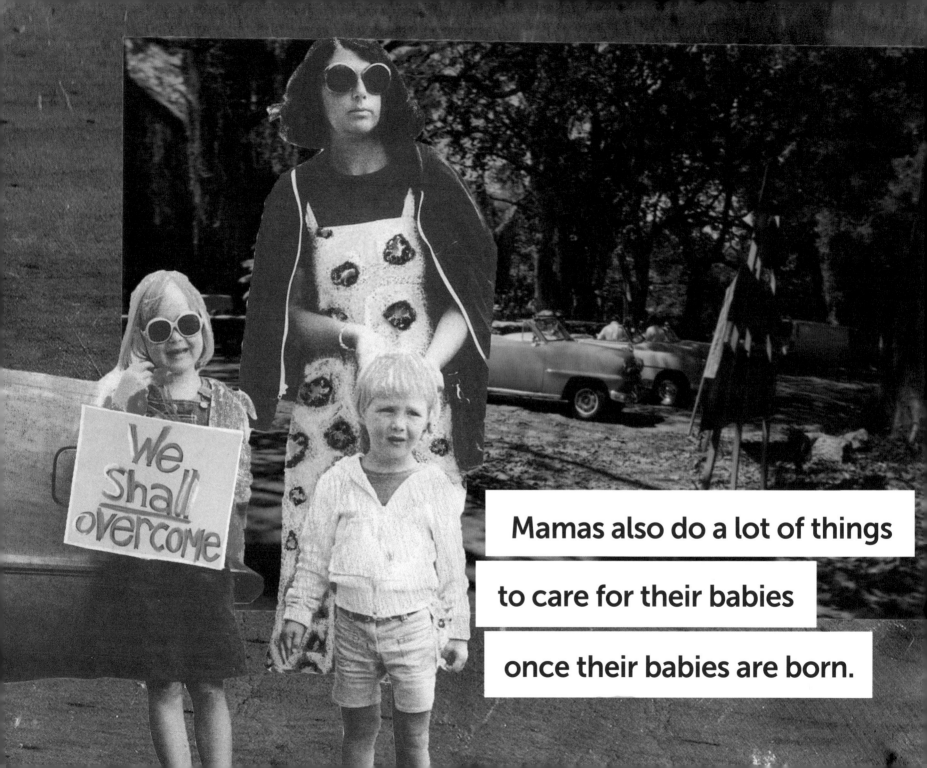

Mamas also do a lot of things to care for their babies once their babies are born.

Some mamas stay home with their babies all day long.

It's hard work!

Some mamas do other kinds of work to care for their babies.

They use their bodies in different ways.

Some mamas use their arms

to clean other people's houses.

Their work helps their babies grow.

Some mamas use their heads to make big ideas.

Their work helps their babies thrive.

Some mamas use their hands to till the green land.

And some mamas use their eyes

to fly planes all around the earth.

Their work helps their babies dream big.

Some mamas do work that needs special clothing.

Some people call these special clothes "uniforms."

Some uniforms are big and baggy.

Some uniforms even have special shoes.

Mamas who dance, just like mamas who clean

and think and farm and fly,

use their whole bodies

to care for their babies.

Mamas who dance,

just like other mamas,

have bodies that love their babies.

Mamas have arms for hugging

and heads for telling bedtime stories

and hands for making good things to eat

and eyelashes for butterfly kisses.

Mamas who stay home and mamas who dance

and mamas who clean and think and

farm and fly

are often tired at the end of the day.

Mamas work hard to care for their babies.

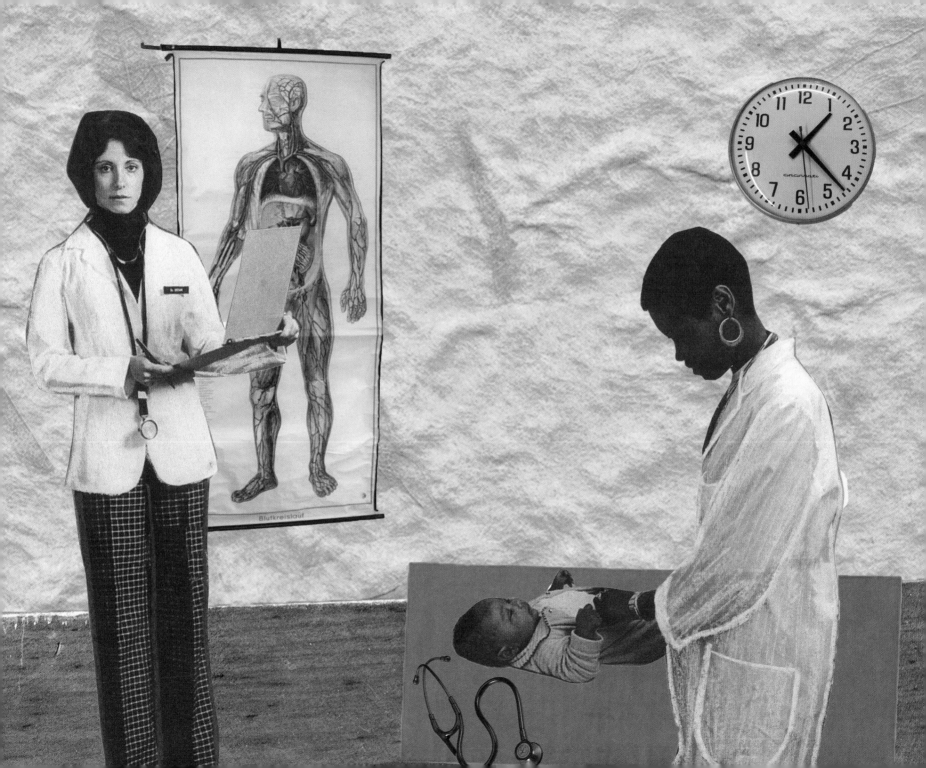

What are the special ways

that your mama cares for you?

THE END